THE LEAF AND THE MARBLE

Also by Iain Crichton Smith from Carcanet

Selected Poems
A Life
Ends and Beginnings
Collected Poems
The Human Face

Iain Crichton Smith

THE LEAF AND THE MARBLE

CARCANET

This is for Donalda
with love and gratitude.

First published in 1998 by
Carcanet Press Limited
4th Floor, Conavon Court
12-16 Blackfriars Street
Manchester M3 5BQ

A CIP catalogue record for this book
is available from the British Library
ISBN 1 85754 400 5

The publisher acknowledges financial assistance
from the Arts Council of England

Set in 10pt Bembo by Bryan Williamson, Frome
Printed and bound in England by SRP Ltd, Exeter

Part One

(1) *The Green Leaf*

My doughty one,
when I think of you
I think of light leaves in Rome
above the marble-
green leaves, green leaves!

As Michaelangelo
on his shaky ladder
so I also admire
courageous fire
fiercely blossoming.

My love,
you believe
that luck will feed us
as meagre saints
hold out their gifts
from empty cupboards.

Not the statues,
no, not the statues,
those imperial riders –
no, but the green leaves
of early April.

Out of the darkness
I rise once more
putting on my blossoms,
and you are there,
a loyal candle.

In the hetacombs of Rome
and at Monte Cassino
so many of the dead,
the young, the ancient,
the crazed, the innocent,
whom the stone imprisons.

In the old damp walls
the martyred Christians.

But the Spring prevails
over the marble –
this shadow of the leaf,
this heartbreak green.

No, not the caparison
of majestic Caesar's
power-stricken hauteur.

But your frail moon,
wavering, shy,
over the dark Tiber.

The young wolves fed
at their lean dam

and I at times
have rested my rhymes
at your hopeful hostelry.

Courage, I am sure,
is the first of virtues

as among the libraries
of arid Ephesus
I saw the poppies
glowing among stones

or at Pompeii
among the ashes
a stubborn lion.

None shall be saved
who doesn't have courage.

As I am your judge
you have that power
which is beyond literature
and our screens of stories.

I come back again
to that bright green leaf
which is stronger than marble.

Rome may die,
as the slavering tribes
ache for its larder.
But that is all foam
if as the sun goes down
the emperor does not burn
in the light of love.

Let him recline
among spurious manuscripts,
how can he survive
in that acid air
of poisonous violins
without the passionate, clear,
gift of a companion.

So many statues,
heavy and firm.
So many riders
fixed in that stone
of determined time.

And the bridges tremble
among the daffodils.

Nevertheless
what without courage,
unwavering candle,
can be accomplished

as the dark Tiber
with its wolf-grey waves
is steadily flowing.

The leaf, the leaf!
April is here
with its constant shuttle.

And love is your
loyal imperative,
as hand in hand
we stroll through this grand

repertoire of scenes,

these pagan oracles
and pipe-playing fountains.

You pull me
out of
the deepest grave
with your bubbling music.
You do not let the antique
overwhelm you
or the helmets
of the dour legions

over whose shaded
and mortal faces
the green leaves play.

Play me my orchestra
of divine feeling
for April is here
and the grave is opened
and I see you there

my dear green leaf
which beyond art
is the gift of life.

O yes, O yes,
my hungry eyes
see this synthesis

though I do not despise
this weighty stone
from Carrara's shrine.

This leaf still plays
in front of the vast
marble arrays.

(2)

Seize it, seize it.
O it will not stay
and that is the mystery
just as imperious
as helmets and spears
among the roses
and the machine-made legion
among the judas
with its flowering sprays.

Slim as a faun
in the heaviness of Rome
I see you running
and you are piping
your quotidian pipe
and water is turning
over and over
among these frozen
forces of power.

Even were the lions,
composed of gaunt flame,
coppery imperium,
to enter the Colosseum
the green leaf will play
about the orchestra
of cruel desire.

And the green leaf will climb
the majestic marble.

Courage remains
the finest virtue
as out of Avernus
we repeatedly climb
into the daylight
where the green leaf plays
and the poet strums
his stony lyre

as he ascends
to the Colosseum
where the coppery lions
rasp their fierce tongues

slavering, furious.
As also Mucius

burned his own hand

and Horatius stood
on the shaking bridge
or the legions turned
at a crumbling wall.

Courage, I say,
my precious one
as the laurel grows
among the shades

like the common thistle.
I see you stand
in the strumming wind.
Rome is built

day after day,
stony, foursquare.
Persephone sways

among the daffodils.
Insoluble,
like Etruscan script
our serious days.

My love, I say
all is equal
among the *res*
mundi
  I've seen you take

a beggar in
from the wild sad road.
Praise O praise
generosity

and also courage,
the leaf that plays
untheatrically
among the operas

and difficult dramas
of our days.
Praise O praise
the local shires

we etch from the blaze
of blue and green.
In ruinous Rome
the poppies nosed

the arid stone.
Or at Pompeii
the fresco shows
cupids and fauns,

a bird on a vase,
a Bacchante nude,
an oven and mill
before the lethal

acid poured down
to fix us in
our contorted poses.
O like the roses

let us brightly wave.
I see you stroll
with your pleated skirt
as if made of marble

in this shuttling April:

Cave canem
I hear them say
of the thorny days.

But I see you put
in your jewellery box
the virtue of courage.
O beware of the dog

who guards the huge
weight of the dark.
If we face it straight

then the laurel waves.

In the fractured *res*
Orpheus strays

then rises again,

Puella, you are
the bright fresh leaf
of acid green
becoming later

the mulier,
the wife and mother.
Than talent dearer
than Roman coin

heavy and grave
is the leaf of courage,
a lunar portion,
or as Apollo

the sunny bow.
At Pompeii

out of the ashes
the poppies blow.

(3)

The Pompeii
of frozen ideas
let us now leave:
the slumped bodies

under the ash.
O dear was the life
common and clear
that these townsmen lived

as the chariot-wheels
carved their routine
on the daily roads
over which walked

in flowing togas
the magisters,
tribunes and plebs.
Dear those rays,

the smell of bread,
the sparse green olives,

the amoretti
plump and winged

and on this day
the stingless butterfly,

that tiny cloud.

(4)

Dear Lares,
protect our larders,
our loved pictures

hung on the walls.
Protect our wardrobes
with their loose blouses

and flowery dresses.
Protect our libraries
with their fine books.
Let no axe

flourish over us
with frosty blade.
Protect the desk
at which I weave

my arabesques.
Let only be published
the best, the best.

Protect the chairs,
the tables and blue
lips of blue rugs.

And do not let
the darkness cripple
in its ominous ripple

our sunny windows
and colourful gardens
where the azaleas
in mild nooks bloom.

(5)   *The Roads of Rome*

Courage, I say,
is the finest virtue.
For we all shake
more than the marble
which stares about us
from rigorous profiles.

Undeviating roads
the will propels
through marsh and moorland
where among boscage
the wet birds sing.

Through heat and cold
through dry and wet
the road proceeds,
stony, remorseless.

But it does not show
the power of the dark.

These many profiles
with their eyeless gaze
as if blinded by light
do not reveal
the shaking mysterious
deepening haze.

Across Britannia
and wooded Gaul
the roads are driven,
stone by stone.
The local gods
are shaken away
from branch and twig,
from their secret heaven.

And the will drives on.

Birds are scattered
out of their nests.
Their naked eggs
are now uncovered.
Through oozing mud
in rain and frost's
imperious crown
the emperor drives
his ruthless chariot.

The demons die
in a hiss of rain.

Bones are unturfed.
Into the air
there's a whirr of wings
of scaly fire.

And the road drives on.
Past Hades itself
at the foggy roadside
that giant cave
with its arrogant shades

of Aeneas and Dido
and huge Achilles.
The road drives on
scattering protean
feathers and leaves.

In the white dust
I see the helmets
of the legions flashing.
Bottomless quarries
are white as ghosts.

And the will drives on.

But courage, I tell you,
it does not speak
of the shaking dark
and the major lyric
that rises and falls.

It does not tell
how the world shakes
how the scenes flicker,
how on both sides
of the road there is heard
a secret snicker,
how on both sides
there is untamed nature,
and quaking bogs
re-form and pucker.

And the road drives on.
But Hades remains —
its bluish veins
and its changing videos.

Hold the green leaf
in front of you
just like a torch
as forward you go
lit by its glow
among the voices,
the sibilant noises,
the snakelike hisses,
the mosses, neuroses,
in a place without glass.

And the road drives on.

And frightened you hear
the sounds of water
ghostly yet clear

And in their hauteur

the ghosts are standing,
changing and bending,
always beyond
the adamant will.

(6)

And this is Hades, the maze of catacombs, the cupboards of the dead. And
here also is a picture of a bird pecking at a bowl of fruit. Here is the
hiss of snakes, the fathomless wolf-coloured twilight, the shifting
panoramas of the heroes without substance.
This is Hades for which courage is needed, where the collars of bone are
stored.
Do not be lost in the labyrinth, find your way back.
Let the light of the ordinary day pour down on you,
let the hisses and the noises be erased.
Enter the shadowless video.

20

(7) *In the Garden*

In the garden I see you
beside the azaleas,
beside the clematis,
among the daisies.

Heal us, dear blaze,
from the seething black.

Our colourful days!

Daffodil, primrose,
tulip, crocus,
no hocus pocus
from these magicians.

How Hades fuels
those innocent fires,
those swaying comely
sinuous flowers.

Hades propels
these impermanent petals.
From infernal cells
they hesitate upward.

No light without dark,
no god without devil,
no good without evil.
The technicians know
that we need the dark.

The leaf, the marble,
the mortal, immortal,
transient, eternal.

So you bend to the earth
with your gardening gloves
protecting your hands
from the rose thorns.

21

And on the stone
butterflies settle.
There's grass on the spade's
luminous metal.

Under the glamour
is poisonous Hades
with its swarms of worms.

Under the face
astoundingly cruel
sunny and pure
the storms of ambition,
limitless power,
imperial venom.

Under the bouquet
the exploding flame.

The muscular roots
develop in darkness,
though we can show
Michaelangelo
dusty and white
rise to his quarry.

As art and ourselves
are haunted by wolves
snapping at flesh
bloody and vicious.

The wolves sit
at our picnic tables.
They face us and they
snap at the plates.

And Rome must suckle
even from these
tribes of wild beasts
as music too towers
from the inharmonious
and as the flowers
shine from the dark.

The wolf's green eyes
are scouring our days
and the red rose sways
out of the dark

and Cerberus barks
sharply, all ways.

(8)

When everything trembles, only love holds it together.
Rome is an act of the will, but the leaf protects us.
Day after day, year after year, Rome with its stony walls and statues is
built above a cage of wolves.
But love is not an act of the will.
No legions can defend or destroy love.
When the walls fly apart, when the horizons shimmer, only love can save
us.
Day by day it towers over us, with its forum, its atria, its columns.
We are inside its massive shadow.
And when Rome falls only the leaf can save us, the leaf of pathos, of
love, of the quotidian.
Its lightness is serious, its play is real.
Iron will not be our breastplate when the horizon shimmers.
Go into the catacomb bearing your wavering leaf.

(9)

The leaves are stronger than the gods, stronger than stone.
The fresh light leaves of love in the Campagna, under a blue sky.
O to be in Rome now that spring is here, now that April is a shadowy
play, is a drama playing over walls, over helmets, over statues, the theatre
of the green leaves.
My love, this is our frail horoscope,
in spite of the drumming funereal Tiber,
in spite of the river which has drowned so many in its poisonous green.
My love, this is our April.
And surely I hear the chaffinch and the cuckoo.
I see the leaf twinkling, the fresh green lively leaf.

(10)   *Dido and Aeneas*

Rome stood up like a wall
and pulled you
from her.

The dark significant profile,
cave of lightning,
that magnificent circle,

Queen of the night.
City of the day,
male and soldierly.

And the god commanded,
This is your task,
not that wayward music,

wavering, indulgent.
Not that effulgent
moon, but Apollo,

bristly and rayed.
You must proceed
towards your fate

and wrap yourself in
the shade of
Rome,

that colossal imperium.
The will, the will,
it must not tremble

like the fresh green leaf,
it must be marble,
imperative.

The sails tremble
over the sea's
blue heat haze,

the fire trembles
just like Apollo's
commanding blaze.

My love, my love,
far from the armour,
imperative,

the quivering sail
in the sea's ring,
passionate beat

of the pulsing waves,
sparkling graves
of a lost love.

For the will must raise
its adamant walls.

Rome is our cost,
our official brute
masonical labyrinth,

bureaucratic mound
against the hyacinth's
vulnerable haze.

The dear *lacrimae*
tremble and play
but the great idea

enchants our days.
And the fire of love
burns the horizon.

The fragile sail
is a butterfly
quickly vanishing,

facing towards
the shelter of Rome,
the dark imperium

of power and hate
away from Troy
that also burned,

to Hannibal's face
set in the blaze
of avenging rage.

O all the light
is perpetual blaze
round the fleeing sails.

Where is the leaf?
The leaves of the waves
make an azure book,

a marvellous tale,
a historic story,
transitory

tale that is told.
Rome is thick-walled
and he hides behind

its massive idea.

To you the power
to outface the proud,

though you are proud.
And she is proud,
tall and unbowed,

bouquet of fire,
leaf on leaf
of miraculous life

and creative story.
Passionate, fiery,
she watched the sail's

perfidious journey,
luminous, finite,
minute, scintillant,

from her black threshold
where with a cold
imperious gaze

haughty and Roman
she never will smile
among the asphodel

though she wears like a scarf
her brilliant leaf.

The green leaf plays
on the victim's hard
and absolute sword.
He'll not outstare
that haughty profile,
he who hid in the haze

and tangled betrayal
of Rome's strict cage
of fire and light

and ponderous walls,
murders and coils
of wolf-like circles,

twilight of deaths,
suicides, myths,
homicides, wreaths.

And Scipio rears
on his smoky horse.
Carthage, he says,

'*delenda est.*'
All is a vast
circle of fire,

of poisonous power.
And you, my dear,
are watching the sail's

winking withdrawal
over the sea's
luminous plain.

But your heart is broken.
The leaf, the leaf
is suddenly shaken

but it still remains
in its frail pathos
against the marble's

memento mori.
Gaiety, sorrow,
delicate, various.

Rome's stone will not
show us the groves
of creative growth

of spontaneous leaves.
Its roads are the will's
dispassionate travels

over wayward belief.
Against the grave
marble, the leaf

in its delicate pathos.
The variorum
of wavering April

transcending the will.
She burns as the sail
burns,
          sacrificial sizzle

And the sail draws away
into permanent exile.
Among the marble

she's a star, a moon,
my nocturnal scene
of leaf and of moon-
struck nightingale.
My Dido, my love,
my dearest profile

invented leaf
of marvellous story,
pathetic, transitory
queen over all.

(11)

The story is vul-
nerable, mobile.

The wayward tale
winds through the
minatory

imperial wall.
The leaves will play
in shadowy April.
These will sustain
us, essential bread.

Out of the dead
ideas of Rome,
of Pompeii

the fresh leaf trembles.
Its brilliant twinkles
keep us alive

in our hazy days.
By the side of the road's
imperious brute

impulsion onward
the leaf's a quick
and powerful ray,

delicate story,
not mandatory,
this trembling tale

more than the marble
on which is inscribed
a deep-fixed script.

As among stone
I saw the poppy's
bright-red wine

foliate sign.
And though Rome may rise
huge and imperious

and spread its shade
over local shrine
and parochial ruin

it will not win
for the heart has days
when the *lacrimae re-*
rum mist the high walls
and rise like a crucial
haze on our souls

that no animals
in brutal displays
will solve, will solve.

And the haunting profile
of Dido slants
over the tenements

and bridges of Rome,
a moon, a leaf,
a sign of this life
that will not fail

our cowardly sail.

31

(12)

Who would descend
into that dark
from the wayward day

voluntarily,
his slender lyric
his only protection

against that Rome
of fiendish roads
and viperish lanes.

Who would not wear
that leaf-coloured sail,
a becalmed angel

in all that weight
of grief and dark,
that world of devil-

ry and pain,
and crooked Pluto
among his hoard

of gold and lead.

And who would not
when that time is past

rise like a leaf
emerald-fresh
into the light

where there are no ghosts,
only the nests
of vernal birds

with their sky-blue eggs,
the springlike garden
which was the Eden

of Adam and Eve
before they're expelled
in a storm of leaves

but now are fresh
among the various
blazes of rose,

daisy, azalea,
and all the marvellous
and airy blooms.

Who would not hold
the breezy leaf
in his darkened hand

as on a lost
wind the imperium
of traditional Rome
disperses like smoke.

(13)

Out of Avernus
I steadily climb
bearing a leaf

so tremulous
in a flood of light
and here I greet

you in your fresh
leaf-coloured shirt
or about the house

your flowery blouse.
The tenderness
of this wavering breeze

how ever express,
or behind our reason
that Rome of dark,

vast and compressed,
as towards you now
I bear this leaf,

my joy and my grief.
Out of the grave
of flickering Hades

I joyfully rise
after these scenes
that hurt my eyes,

and terrified me,
the running wolves,
the emptying graves.

And now I bear

my quivering leaf
as an angel might
on the new found earth

or the gift of a rose.
So out of the gross
dark of Avernus

I freely bear
my gift of a leaf

from my renaissance
this light bright leaf.

Love, let you rise
as Venus might
from her leaf-shaped shell

in a storm of roses.
O primavera
out of the darkness,

clear mild spring
of the vernal goddess
all in a ring

of blooms and posies.
Or in modest grave
and serious dress

suitable to
a Presbyterian
(not Mediterranean)

severe land

Still
let the wind
be sweet and various

a million-scented
inventive breeze
of eternal days

fresh and hilarious
with a secret laughter
like a pulsing haze.

I put you in
my leaf-ringed diary
so large and airy

and these dark tombs
with their maze of worms
suddenly vanish

against this fresh
untarnished leaf
as out of darkness

I quickly step
into the chain
and the design

inwoven thus
of emerald *Amor*
Vincit Omnia

O not a trinket
but against insomnia
a holy cure

And so I bear
my renaissance leaf
away from mediaeval

theology
away from the bony
catacombs

and skeletons

into a sky
of airy blue

not Presbyterian
but Mediterranean

and pagan venue.

(14)

And so I have traced,
yes, I have traced
the secret at last

it is Rome that is
the Presbyterian
uncreative place,

it is Rome that has
the massive ponderous
unlifelike gaze

with its deaths and spies,
its historical bones,
its skeletons

of cobwebbed skulls.
It is Rome that dulls
bright nature's smile

with its heavy marble
and stony designs.
It is Rome that has

that fixed ingrained
Presbyterian gaze,
that marmoreal

visage of guile
that bends over all
unlike the tall

gaze of great Dido,
changing, spectral.

It's the leaf that is

what I now sniff
on a fine day
which is eternal

because it strays
about the nostril
and sensitive profile.

The leaf, the sail!

And you in your
domestic dress
and self-possessed

and clear Dutch light
are my desire.

And on your blouse
are flowers and light.

Rome, farewell,
from this airy place
that I have found,

this pagan heaven
and airy garden
far from your dull

and ponderous smile.

O pagan days
to you I rise
out of Avernus'

hinged skeletons
and caches of bones,
presbyterian,

O I'll atone
for the will's design
by the wayward shrine

that I make for you
in that storm of roses,
that pretty shell,

so vulnerable.
And so I tell
that this is the best,

the vulnerable.
And all the rest
heavy and still,

made of hard marble.

But the wayward flesh
though not eternal
is the delicate bell
that freshly rings.

O the terrestrial
is the eternal.
That is what clings

to my soaring lyric
like patient grass.
We rise from gross

considerings

like the rose-lit spray
of Botticelli.

We're our own May
if we so wish.

And this I say

though Rome fall down
with its Colosseum
and brutal games

and the lion holds
us in its mouth
in its yellow folds

we always escape.

Your quotidian pipe
enchants me still,

veritas amoris

Out of stone quarries

the dear green earth's

amazing rays.

Part Two

(1)

In this clear air
you take your basket over
to the village.
        There is a sparkle
of leaves everywhere.
It is spring
and glamour
of birds on branches as
in an illuminated picture
by monks.
        The water
is pure, and the sky also
after its red and black veins
of last evening, a factory
of beaten metal.
        There is no cloud
of wandering exile.
        The sparkles
burn from windows and gates
and the daffodils are ablaze.
        O hope
that others might share it, might
from marsh and dull brick
share it.
        The fire
of the sun everywhere, vernal,
diurnal, the passion
of the swallows.
        And the pendent
nests with their freights
of delicate eggs.
        The gorse
blazing like a shield, bright
and yellow.
        My hand
is alive with the fire, the wing
of a bird speeding.
        This diary

of airy brilliant events –
        this sky.

(2)

You through the sparkle
bear your unadorned
springy basket.
        The dazzle
burns from the leaves, from the roof
signalling red.
        I
meditate foxes, nature's
anthology moving
among green trees.
        Peace
be with you, shalom
of our unbiblical days.
Glitter from mirror
of loch.
        And the rowan
will bend over water. The
blood of fertility. The moon
of a fine white.
        Now
the spring of renewal
hesitating towards summer. Fire
reflects from the leaves. The gnome
stands up in the garden, red
among the spades and the rakes. So
the bowed gardener
sparkles in fire.
        I hear
the music of swallows.
        The azaleas
will blaze, and the bush
of blue rhododendrons, and the bees

44

buzz among the clematis.
        Fatalities
are here and now in this
momentary accidental
pouring of light.
            Let us not part
from heart-breaking nature.

(3)

        Freed from the
weight of Rome, the deaths
of Egypt.
        The ring of spring
is dazzling. The tombs
are too heavy for the light,
the maze
of bureaucracy. The
sketches and functions of leaves
so faint, so delicate.
        Birds too
perch on their fine
provisional branches, their beaks
yellow and fresh. The twigs
are hieroglyphics.
        Rome will burn
in the sea of sparkles, this
candelabra of flame.
        Over the flood
races the leaf-like sail.

(4)

The leaf, the sail
vulnerable as the shadow
pursues them, lies
massively over the water,
burns like a burning ship.
        The curve
of the sail so lissom, the
curve of the leaf.
        Ponderous Rome
opens its wolf-like jaws, takes
them into its ashen stomach,
Pompeii of dead forms.
        Be free
O individual soul,
be lively.
        Flight of the swallow
over our local roofs.

(5)

The local
be with us in its
harmonious sparkle, the general
be a cast-off mountain of dark.
        The deer
are a delicate, pure,
sketch and indigenous profile.
        Pull
us out of the tomb, out of the
haze and vagueness of Hades
into the local light.
        You are walking
at the moment along this road,
a girl
hauling two large black dogs.

(6)

But nevertheless the local
transcends the dark pile.
          The till
rings with our local money.
And the wine bottles
stand upright in local shops.
          The mortal
will clothe us.
          Our loaves
are fresh with the smell
of the local oven, not the prestige
of Rome.
          I speak
with the mouth of a local bird
resting a moment
on a warm temporary stone.

(7)

The intricate leaf unfurls
and tells its tale.
          It is a deer's
questioning of the *res
mundi*, an antler's precise
thrust from the grove.
          The grave
is the heaviness of Rome.
          A swarm
of bees will enliven.
          The local
is sparkle of *res*, parochial
candelabra.
          The rook
caws from the causeless tree.

(8)

Indigenous diurnal projects
and fading galleries.
The sagacious owl cries
among the leaves.
        I see
a trembling of
things,
the *lacrimae rerum* sparkling,
fading and growing.
        My pleasure
rests on a twig, heaven
is here, is here, precisely
on this branch, this moment.
        The breeze
brings us its perfume, and the gorse
is a lingo of yellow.
        The *Georgics*
please more than the *Aeneid*
Not from the large
empire of Rome, the gloom
of the catacombs
but just outside the cave
where the lightning flashes,
the wink of the leaf, the
minute sparkle of the provisional.
        The rook
caws from the roof, fading.
        The owl
wise in its moment clasps
a bouquet of rays.

(9)

Clear fresh morning, I remember you
though my head is thick
with the shade
of wavering Hades.
            The tree winks
with its weight of leaves and
our gate welcomes strangers.
            Let Virgil
and Dante enter
like beggars or like
tourists from the street, asking
directions among the radiance. We are
here, waiting, in this day
that passes. The rabbits
race below the leaves. You touch
your togas ornamented
with green. Sit here
on this bench, I will bring you
a cup of pure water, after the
light has touched your gowns.
Look at the leaves. It is right
to gaze on this foliage, the light
and luminous green. You wear
the shifting marble of Rome and the
ashes of Hades. Here there is none
such, the leaves
are random, arbitrary, and the weeds
thrust among them, demanding
their own lives. Also the local
graves are crumbling
and the parson
walks absentmindedly among them.
            Children
can be heard shouting
as they hold up the gnome they have found
beside the well, among the foliage,
the ricocheting sparkle, and their games
are echoes of our lives. See,

everything is finite, my dear
marmoreal masters, the agonised
ricti. Here rest
at this provisional hostelry before
resuming your journey. I brush
ash from your cloaks. I brush
from your cloak the feuds
and murders of clerisy. Better
stay here for a while before
entering that mortuary. Let these dreams
fade, these hellish videos.
The sun sparkles on the leaf.
We are here finitely, we are not
frozen Pompeii.

(10)

        Like children
we turn over the coloured
pages, the scenes of the everyday.
The horses
and dolls are around us, toys
that we perish among, and cherish
as the sun goes down. The
children are concentrated, in a
closing of lips, of attention. The gnome
rises freshly from the well.
Holy holy holy the things
of everyday, sparkles stream from them.
They are interrupted by
marble and Roman statues. We raise
these to remember, we raise things to be
ideas and stones in the stream. We
overpower the leaves with them but
the leaves are eternal, nature is
eternal, pathos is eternal, and the wheel
outlasts us in spite of
riders fixed on their marble.

The shadows
of Hades flicker at the gates
where the leaves are sparkling.
Pick one, bear it with you like a torch, hold
onto its freshness. We are
naked cherubs that are clothed, we
are naked beings.
In order to remember
we raise our statues of stone
against that terrestrial sparkle. We
would forget but for the
marble that holds us. The leaf
freshens in our hands.

(11)

Masters
we have not yet faced the sparkle,
that orphan pathos, the leaf
that leans from nature. Not yet
have we suffered the look that is
endlessly plotless, we have not yet
been burned by the power of the leaf.
Hell is not here, it is elsewhere
among murderous corridors. It is
Dido eternally dark, watching the
receding sail. But tell us O tell us
how we can bear the acid
power of the leaf, how we can bear
the venom of the immediate, its scent,
the fox that runs across the field
in its flickering red. The leaf
will teach us, that bears
the warmth of the sun, the veined
charts of the day. Let
Hades be packed away, masters,
and the skulls of the past, the

tortures of ancient feuds, the rings
of traditional fires.

  Let us walk, magisterial geniuses, in the light
that tricks us with beginnings, the cries
of the children on the shores
of the everchanging real. The sail
glitters and sparkles, the mussel-coloured
glittering finite sail.

(12)

         More terrible
even than Rome is this
encounter with the leaf, at which
we do not worship. More terrible
this lack of dogma, this light, this
unstructured library. More
innocent this unjudged fire, this
scent of the arbitrary. At night
there are millions of jewels, a shop
burning in space.
         The dogmas
die between planets. Hear ye,
inordinate *res* who are the
herald of the present. I stand
and sing open-mouthed, the
bucket of cinders in my hand.
The world streams
over and over rejoicing, life
is the meaning of life. We turn
page after page without plot. We
make our own plots, and the leaf
defeats us, it is veined
with its green sap, is found
at the very dark lip of Hades, our
package of memories. It is fearful.
See how it brilliantly sparkles. The owl
fixes its scholarly glasses.

(13)

How tiny the leaf
against the shadow of Rome, of
ideology. And yet
how precious. I touch it
and it burns my hand.
The provisional
is frightening. The stomach tightens
thinking of it. Do only routine
and bureaucracy save us? Also
Hades is terrifying, the shift
of the horizon, the schizophrenic
doublings.
    Still,
the leaf can save us, if we
brood on it ardently, without
proscription.
    Hold it,
like a torch, Dante, hold it,
sensitive Virgil, it
saves, it is the beat
of the everyday, when everything shifts,
when the historical
crimes have to be paid for,
and the skull howls.
    My leaf,
my sail, mark of the present,
transitory coming and going, badge
of the present.
    Love, my love,
leaf shining so greenly
against the green-eyed wolf.

(14)

Before there was Rome, there was the leaf.
Before the shadow fell, there was the light.
Before the marble there was the tree.

The little forlorn stone sat among the thistles.
The thistles themselves did not wear crowns.

The little begging children hovered by the road
before there was Rome.

The rain fell, and the Tiber
reflected the sky and the grass
before there was Rome.

Before the maze was created,
before Caesar projected his programmes,
the judas tree illuminated the air,
and there was the leaf.

The helpless things were there trembling
the gipsy in her torn dress
wept by the Tiber.

Before Rome came to protect us and enslave us.
And the marble heads stare from the wall
with their empty sockets.

(15)

Rome towers over us, in its labyrinthine passages we are trapped, we
cannot escape the grief of its dungeons, though outside the prisoner's
window the green leaf trembles.
Oh it was towards Rome that you sailed, Aeneas, in your ship that ignored
the winking of waves. You carried your father on your back out of Troy
blazing like a ruby.

And you entered the terrible idea, power, terror, voyeurism, the gladiator
shaken in the jaws of the lion.
Senators with their stony faces glared over the arena. In the marshes the
noise of their midnight intrigues.
While the leaf trembled at the window, the provisional and poetic
shimmered.
The roads of the will levelled Nature, and the tremulous animals fled
from you. And your ideology solidified into icons, and you taught us
copious bleeding.
And we could not weep because of you.
And your clerks signed the timetables of millions while the fresh leaf
trembled. The leaf sparkled as your infamous chariots despoiled
Carthage, on the road to Hades, towards its smoke, towards the lovers
handcuffed together in inseparable iron.
And the provisional faded, and could not withstand you, and the *lacrimae*
trembled like dew.
And feminine Vergil succumbed to the bronze of Augustus.

(16)

Jupiter, you brutally seized them.
You were the thunder of the absolute.
Did you not feel the trembling as you bent your head towards their
mouths? As a mouse might tremble in the grip of the owl and in the
infinite nocturnal jewellery. Your eagle wings outspread them, you did not
feel the mortal trembling.
For your will was absolute, Rome was absolute, it worked out the iron
meaning of itself.
And it had no memory of the injured, it did not start up wide-eyed in the
night.
It raised its banners over the trembling lands and villages: its legions
marched to the hollow rhythm of drums.
It laughed at the bloodied gladiator struggling in the net.
And the sail frail as a leaf winked in the million twinkles of
waters, traitor, betrayer of the Dido who died in the ruby-red fire.

(17)

> *Sunt*
> *lacrimae rerum*
> *mentem mortalia*
> *tangunt.*
>
> The leaf
> trembles in the wind;
> the sail trembles
> on the wave,
> Grief
> trembles in the fire.
> But the
> senators with arrogant *fasces*
> propel history.
> My love,
> the shade of Rome rises
> over us unless afresh
> we judge each day.
> Unless
> April attracts us
> with its shuttle
> of light.
> The blood
> of the gladiator speckles
> the arena, the crowd
> eats him.
> Unless the leaf
> trembles and we are
> where he is dangling.
> The tears
> are the dew trembling
> on the local
> thistle and fern.
> You
> among others I weep for
> in my guilt
> that my sail took you from me
> that your suicidal pyre
> was a perfect star.

          Complexity
of the *res*, the
seriousness
of it.
          To meet them
in Hades perhaps
with their coiffed helmets
cut and grey
among the yellow tide
of asphodel.
          I tremble
in my bed, my shell
so delicate, O slaves
of the will.
          Terrible
the market that we create,
terrible the stare
of the empty coats and the
handkerchiefs that accuse
us.
          O precious
the leaf, but you, Rome,
are abuser of millions.
          Your helmets
that like mussels
adorn the borders.
          Rome
of the riotous mob, concourse
of assassins.
          I tremble
under the millions of stars,
these jewelled populations,
this vibrating universe.
          I ask
pity on my deeds
though not from Augustus.
          The will
indicts us with the straightness
of roads which usurp
the local gods, the marsh's

domestic cry of the peewit.
         Rome,
I abhor you.
           Let me tremble
let my sail tremble,
a diaphanous poppy.

Epilogue

The following poems refer to an Egyptian painting.
It shows the Golden Throne, with King Tutankhamun
and his wife Akhesenamun

(1)

                This moment
my eye rested on
this painting.
                The throne
a delicate lyric blue
on which the lissom curve
of his body rests.
                Their crowns
blue, and a sun blazing
out of the heavens. The throne
as light as a branch, not knowing
the earth.
                Her hand is resting
on his shoulder.
                And their eyes
are fixed on each other.
                Love is here –
the perfect unadorned gaze.
This blueness, it is
calm and silence.
                The hands,
the limbs, are so delicate,
airy, transcendent. The throne
tilts into the air, such a fine
transaction. She touches
him with wonderment, lightly
out of the light, amazed
at finding him there.
                And he also
reflecting her dear eyes.
                Egyptian
heaviness is gone, the custom
of death.
                This is an idyll
freed even of gravity, the will
untrammelled, lifted into the air
of a lucky finding.

(2)

       No room
for one word, in this
exquisite air, this price-
less aether.
       Against the gold–
wrought precious background
these two
         are designed,
negligent
         of the ponderously yellow.
In this invented obsession
there's a chain
that lightly binds them together
in this airy blue.

(3)

       Domestic
bliss is implicit
here, the days
passing, in the blaze
of the sun's rays.
       The *res*
mundi are arranged
round you, the eyes
crossing the border
between which the sun pours
an ardent blossom.
       The body
weightlessly sits
on the tremendous
authority of the throne
so lightly taken, as if
death were not an Egyptian.

Who can speak
of this moment; who can
between this king and queen
set a word?

(4)

            I return
over and over
to this obsessive
painting, to this meeting
as if freshly composed
in the astonishing
given.
            The curve,
fluent and feminine,
of the young Pharaoh,
liberated from weight
and the fate
of Egypt.
            And the light
sketch of the chair,
so finely azure.
            Time is elsewhere –
this vision is so pure
that the two are like flowers
growing,
            convergent
on the ordinary day
with its clear rays
in which as in a story
they meet each other,
transcendent.
            I cannot say
what this moment portends
as if examining the jewellery
of the exposed soul.

(5)

So
love is a finding, in this
air of summer, a literal
coming upon, as a bird
coming into the world
and finding
the faintly provisional.
This is the moment
wordless, perfect,
a coming upon
the finite flesh, the pliant
plant-like body, resting
on a project of throne.
One cannot will this, it is
the given.
It is the
axiom of an ardent
geometry. Such precious
grace and precise
invention.
The slanted
agate eyes at the gate
of seeing, the hands
trustfully resting, everything
resting in love as in
an element,
an
almost questioning wonderment,
elegantly so.